This book will be used by

_____ *and* _____

Prayer Partners and Marriage Partners

To Mary and Bob, sister and brother,
  whose love we cherish,
  whose faith we admire,
  we dedicate this book.

A PRAYERBOOK FOR HUSBANDS AND WIVES

A PRAYERBOOK FOR HUSBANDS AND WIVES
Partners in Prayer

Copyright © 2000 Ruthanne and Walter Wangerin, Jr. All rights reserved.

Except for brief quotations in critical articles or reviews, no part of this book may be reproduced in any manner without prior written permission from the publisher. Write to: Permissions, Augsburg Fortress, Box 1209, Minneapolis, MN 55440.

Scripture quotations are from the New Revised Standard Version Bible, copyright © 1989 by the Division of Christian Education of the National Council of the Churches of Christ in the U.S.A. and used by permission.

Excerpts marked LBW are from Lutheran Book of Worship, copyright © 1978.

Cover photography copyright © 2000 PhotoDisc. Used by permission.
Cover design by Marti Naughton
Interior design by Timothy W. Larson

Library of Congress Cataloging-in-Publication Data

Wangerin, Ruth.
    A prayerbook for husbands and wives: partners in prayer / Ruthanne and Walter Wangerin.
    p.cm.
    Includes index.
    ISBN 0-8066-4062-6 (alk paper)
    1. Spouses—Prayer-books and devotions—English. I. Wangerin, Walter. II. Title.

BV4596.M3 W36 2000
242'.844—dc21   00-041623

The paper used in this publication meets the minimum requirements of American National Standard for Information Sciences—Permanence of Paper for Printed Library Materials, ANSI Z329.48-1984. ♾ ™

Manufactured in the U.S.A.   AF 9-4062

04   03   02   01   00   1   2   3   4   5   6   7   8   9   10

A PRAYERBOOK
FOR HUSBANDS AND WIVES

Partners in Prayer

Ruthanne and Walter Wangerin, Jr.

Augsburg
MINNEAPOLIS

CONTENTS

FOREWORD: ON MARRIAGE AND PRAYER

THANNE AND I HAVE BEEN MARRIED FOR THIRTY-TWO YEARS. Vigorous years. Our marriage has been a story of calm days, common days, days of a sudden and blinding transcendence; we've sinned and confessed and forgiven; there have been trips and children, emergency rooms, schoolrooms, courtrooms, and through it all—through the daily round of human duties—faith. Our faith, yes; but more surely than that, the faithfulness of heaven.

God has been the deeper love and the ground of our marriage, always.

But I myself—I did not always acknowledge that. Nor did I always take advantage of the sweet communion of prayer.

Thanne has. And it was Thanne who persuaded me to pray out loud with her.

Within days of our wedding, I began studies at Concordia Seminary in preparation for ministry, and Thanne began her profession as a teacher. Those were hard times for her. Often, in visible stress, she would say, "Wally, we should pray together."

I didn't disagree. But neither did I actually agree.

I'm not sure why. Perhaps because, though my father was a pastor, I never experienced spontaneous prayer before. We'd only prayed formal prayers—as Thanne and I did at mealtimes now. And I think I was embarrassed by the danger of prayer: revealing myself, inverting the truer truth of myself before Jesus and Thanne together.

But in those days I was an angry young man, angry for causes I couldn't see—so neither could I see the anger in me. Thanne did, of course. Thanne suffered my fits of gloom. And sometimes I saw that: her suffering. And when I knew that I had hurt her, I grieved.

"Thanne," I said. "Thanne," I begged her in the heat of my shame, "what can I do to make it up? What can I do to prove I love you?"

One day, when I was in deepest need of her forgiveness, the opportunistic Ruthanne said, "Pray with me, Wally. Pray out loud with me."

I was caught. I could not avoid the issue.

"Okay."

But I was the seminary student. I knew about God. So I took us into the bedroom and said we should lie down on the bed. We did. Side by side.

But I felt breathless. Nervous. "Wait!" I cried. I jumped up and turned off the light. Somehow this praying thing seemed as awkward and exposed as the first time we made love together.

"Now, then." I went first.

I gathered my thoughts, cleared my throat, then, in the darkness, began to fashion a formal, literate prayer. Petitions. Bible verses. I surprised myself. My voice grew strong. See, Thanne? See? I can do this after all. I succeeded very well in sounding like a preacher in the pulpit.

When I finished there was a silence. Had she fallen asleep?

No, she hadn't.

Quietly Thanne began to pray, with no more force or formality than when she talks softly to me at night. But she was talking to Jesus. It seemed as if I weren't even there. Jesus was close, intimate to her. Jesus was all. And I felt a little like a peeping Tom, not so much hearing her prayer as overhearing it.

I was ashamed. My brazen prayer was only a crashing cymbal next to the common honesty of her language. And I realized that I had, in effect, prayed to her, prayed for her approval, while she was praying to Jesus, for Jesus' blessed response.

And then, still in her tender and sacred conversation, Thanne began to tell the Lord Jesus about "Wally." About me. As if I were so important that Jesus should take care of me. And in that moment, in the darkness, I started to cry.

What a gentle love my wife displayed: first for Jesus, and then for me—but within that divine love her marital love glowed with a holy light, shining Christ on me. We three were woven into a graceful, tough, and sacred whole. I, too: I had entered the intimacy. That's why I was crying.

And all this was done in prayer, through prayer, together, out loud.

Embarrassment became meekness. And the revealing of my truest truths only meant that the whole of me had been invited into the intimacy between my wife and my Lord.

Thanne's lesson has never been lost on me. Prayer is more than the uttering of private words: it's the room we enter together; it is a place where the marriage might dwell a while, protected, candid, consoled—the whole of the marriage in all of its parts, under the love of Jesus.

WW

When our children were young, our son Joseph's illnesses were sometimes accompanied by dangerously high fevers. One evening during family prayer time, our daughter Talitha prayed, "God, please make Joseph get better. And make his temperature go down to zero." I've chuckled often over that prayer through the years, but it taught me something very important: that when, in our weakness, we pray for foolish things, the Holy Spirit interprets and intercedes on our behalf.

Throughout our marriage, there sometimes has been difficulty in knowing what to pray or even, in our ignorance, praying for foolish things. But I am always encouraged by what Saint Paul had to say about Talitha's prayer: "Likewise the Spirit helps us in our weakness; for we do not know how to pray as we ought, but that very Spirit intercedes with sighs too deep for words. And God, who searches the heart, knows what is the mind of the Spirit, because the Spirit intercedes for the saints according to the will of God" (Rom. 8:26, 27).

In later years, one of our children suffered a difficult transition through adolescence and early adulthood. During those years, I heaved innumerable supplications into the face of God. I prayed daily for the physical and spiritual life of my child. For years I pleaded with God to restore my child. One day I realized that for some time—I don't know how long—I had been praying thanksgiving: thanksgiving for God's intervention, thanksgiving for God's flawless fatherhood. I don't know when or how this transition occurred because, as far as I could tell, circumstances had not changed. What I know now is that the Holy Spirit was interpreting my prayers in ways that I didn't know. The Spirit of God was teaching me how to pray, was placing words in my heart and on my tongue that I was incapable of praying. I came to realize later that it was at this time that a change was beginning in my child's heart as well as my own. The Spirit knew what I could not know and directed my prayer.

This is what happens when we pray. God's great wisdom not only teaches us how to pray, but interprets our prayer and shapes it into what it ought to be. Like children who are unable to form words to ask from their parents, we bring our inarticulate petitions to God. Like children who don't understand the fullness of what they need, we pray in faith. Like children, we pray with full confidence that God will hear. God knows both what we are asking and what is good for us. What we pray is not as important as that we pray. In the asking, our relationship with God grows. And when we pray with our spouse or for our spouse, our bond with each other is strengthened as well.

RW

How to Use This Book

This book offers three distinct opportunities for married couples:

(1) Prayers on many topics (sometimes there are two prayers per topic, one for each spouse; sometimes there is a line-by-line dialogue; sometimes one prayer for both of you). Pray these out loud together, whenever the need and occasion arise. Take time! Sit down. Allow yourselves a devout attitude. Go slowly. Make the expressions and the appeals your own by fitting the prayer to *your* lives.

The index in the back of this book shows you at a glance how many topics these prayers can cover. If you feel the strong need to pray, but are too confused to know the reason, look in the index.

(2) Litanies for repeated occasions (to be used at the beginning of important moments in the marriage—to be used over and over again). Each of these contains its own instructions—but all of them ask you to find a special place in your home for your prayers, devotions, and litanies together.

(3) Directions and suggestions for an annual private retreat, the two of you alone. We urge all married couples to consider the importance of this retreat. Often it was the sweetening—and sometimes the salvation—of our marriage.

In the prayers you will hear our separate voices, husband and wife distinguished from one another. We've made our prayers both personal and universal. But we suggest that you choose which of you will pray a particular prayer the best; just switch the language, replacing *husband* for *wife,* and vice versa.

We've designed the book to last you many years. Even though you will repeat the prayers over and over, you can make them new by referring to the Bible passages bracketed within them. In the beginning, ignore the citations; but the more you pray a particular prayer, the more you'll want to study those passages to enrich the prayer's words and meaning. If you wish, you can base a series of marital devotions upon these prayers, discussing the biblical passages together.

There is no necessary sequence to your use of this book. Choose prayers as they apply; pray each litany at its appropriate time.

Nevertheless, we do suggest that you both, independently, read through the whole book before you begin its regular use. Learn the tools it offers your private worship so that you can make the book your own.

For this reason (and to ease your shared praying) we suggest that you get two copies of the book, one for each of you. You'll want to make notes on your own pages; and you won't have to switch one book back and forth while praying.

Note: We ask each of you to keep two diary-like notebooks: one for personal thanksgivings (see the litany for suppertime), and one to list the things you give to God (see the litany "For the Sabbath"). These books will increase your constant attention to God, and they will serve you well during the annual retreat.

The litanies are meant to act as milestones throughout the journey of your married life, shaping your time, devoting it to the Lord. The "Thanks at suppertime" litany can be used daily; the "For the Sabbath" litany, weekly; the "Before Bible study or devotions together" litany, as regularly as you two determine; the "On an anniversary" litany . . . well, of course.

As we said, we hope that our book becomes your book; that you establish certain prayerful patterns with us in order to fill those patterns with your words, your topics, your needs, your souls.

Therefore, each of the litanies also leads you to language of your own, invites you to discover practices special to the two of you. As you grow confident in these brief moments of worship, introduce gestures and prayerful exchanges that carry the meaning of your own faithful experience.

This collection is not intended to fulfill all of your prayer needs, nor does it presume to be a substitute for your more personal spontaneous prayer. Because this book, by its nature, focuses on your relationship with each other, it does not address the many other facets of your lives as parents or friends or members of a community. It is our hope, however, that it will become a tool for establishing and maintaining a healthy prayer life, strengthening the bond not only between the two of you, but also, together, between the two of you and God.

Walt & Thanne Wangerin

PRAYERS

DAILY LIVING
AS HUSBAND AND WIFE

MARRIAGE ROLES

GOD OF CREATION, you made us man and woman, male and female. You created and blessed our union. You made us different, yet perfectly suited to each other. Still we struggle with defining our roles. We can't always figure out who should be shopping for groceries or doing the laundry or mowing the lawn. We can't always agree on who should call the electrician or take the car in for repairs. We each struggle with finding time to take care of the many family responsibilities we have every day.

Give us your wisdom, Lord, to balance our lives and to define our roles within our marriage. Forgive my self-centeredness when I feel I'm bearing more than my share of the load. Forgive me when I don't carry my share of the responsibilities. Give me the quietness and peace to talk to my *husband* without anger and without blame. Give us both wisdom to know how to divide responsibility, and give us each a spirit of self-giving to ease the burden of the other.

You created us both, Lord. Use your creative hand to form for us a way to equitably divide our duties in peace and harmony. In the name of Jesus. Amen.

RW

HOLY GOD, your image is not in me alone; it's in us both; it's in the living relationship between us, in our marriage, in the way we work together to serve you in your creation (Gen. 1:27-31).

Forgive me when I destroy that image by making demands rather than making consensus with my *wife*.

Let us from that image wisely divide the family work between us according to practical needs rather than pride. Help us to learn how we are helpers that fit one another (Gen. 2:18) rather than laborers forced to work unwillingly, unhappily.

Direct us, Lord, by your presence to divide our duties not according to selfish personal desires but rather according to the family's needs; the spiritual gifts, skills, and talents God has given each of us individually; and with love as the dominant motive.

Finally, Lord, make all the service I give my *wife* and my family be my service and worship unto you, and then it shall be a perpetual expression of joy.

WW

FINANCES

GIVER OF ALL THINGS, you have blessed us with far more than we need in our lives. You have given us shelter and food, clothing and transportation, employment and children. And yet we struggle and sometimes disagree about how we should spend our money. We can't always decide whose needs or wants should have priority. We can't always agree on how much we should spend on Christmas and birthday gifts. We can't always be clear about which charities should receive our gifts. We can't always decide whether we should buy a new car or repair the old one.

Forgive us, Lord, when we forget to thank you for your abundance. Help us to distinguish between what is necessary and what is desired. Cleanse us from the sin of covetousness and direct our decisions about how to spend or save our money. Help us to remember to give to you first and to trust that you will provide the rest. Keep our hearts focused on what is most important—you, our faith, our family. Guard us against greed and the desire to accumulate earthly goods, which are only temporary. Keep our eyes trained on your eternal treasures so that what we have here becomes less important. When we disagree on how our income should be used, remind us of your greatest gift, Jesus, and the poor whom you love. Then show us how to use your gifts wisely and to your glory. Amen.

RW

Before praying, read Deuteronomy 14:22-29. This blessing described in verse 29 means that we will find a holy delight and a sacred satisfaction in the work we do, not that we will make more money.

JESUS, I CONFESS:

I've allowed my concerns about finances to break faith with you, as if money were more important to our survival than your love, your promises, and my obedience. I have sometimes used my control of the family money as a means to control my family. I sometimes believe that because I make the most money I should have the most to say about how we spend it. I think our resources are mine to earn and deserve, not yours to give and oversee for the benefit of all. I see myself as the owner, not as your steward.

JESUS, LET ME BEGIN WITH YOU:

I will obey the Lord's blessed call to tithe all the yield of our labor, for by the tithe, we will "learn to fear the Lord our God always"; I and my household, by serving the Lord, will truly experience joy; and, in return, "the Lord our God will bless us in all the work of our hands that we do."

WW

FRIENDS

DEAR FATHER OF ALL, you put us into families and communities. Thank you for my family—my *husband,* my children, my parents, my brothers and sisters. Thank you also for my family of friends *(if you wish, you may name specific individuals or groups after each description below):*

~ for those who rejoice in the blessings of my spouse and children;
~ for those who share the burdens during difficult times;
~ for those who pray for me when I am suffering;
~ for those who uphold me when I am weak;
~ for those who comfort me when I feel alone;
~ for those who listen when I need advice;
~ for those who share their wisdom;
~ for those who help me keep my marriage vows;
~ for those who encourage me when I become weary;
~ for those who laugh with me when my joy overflows;
~ for those who see the humor in difficult situations.

Thank you for all of my friends, Father, especially those who help to make my marriage strong by being a good friend to me. Amen.

RW

Father, protect our individual and our family friendships:

Since each of us needs a private confidant (even someone with whom to discuss the marriage), keep me from suspicions and foolish jealousies regarding the friend of my *wife*.

At the same time, keep me wise in my own friendships, that I never offer my friends what I've promised my *wife* alone, nor ever take from my friends what is only my *wife*'s to give.

Grant us a community of faithful friends to surround and protect our marriage while sharing our love for you.

Grant us friends with whom we can pray aloud together.

And empower the two of us, individually and together, to be true friends for our friends; and to be friends who reflect your most blessed sort of friendship (John 15:12-15).

Because you are yourself the most faithful of friends, we pray to you with the confidence—the conviction—that you will hear and answer. Amen.

WW

PRIVACY OF SPACE, TIME, THOUGHTS

Dear Jesus, you recognized the need for the human spirit to be replenished in solitude, sometimes going off to be by yourself.

It's hard in my hectic life to find time to be alone. The cares of my family and *husband,* the stresses of my job, the responsibilities of aging or ill parents, the needs of others in my church and community—all of these require my time. But you were busy, too, with people constantly demanding your energy; and yet you took time to find solitude to refresh your spirit.

Remind me of that need to refresh my spirit, and give me the discipline to set aside some time in each day or week for solitude. Teach me the necessity of pulling back from the demands in my life, especially those that draw me away from you. You provided a day of rest for me—a Sabbath. Give me wisdom to use it in the way you intended—for your glory and my renewal. Just as I tithe my earthly goods, help me tithe my time, giving you my firstfruits. In your name. Amen.

RW

Jᴇsᴜs, I ᴄᴏɴꜰᴇss:

My *wife* wanted to be alone today. *She* didn't want to do things with me—and I felt rejected. I confess my self-centeredness. Not everything in *her* life has to do with me.

My *wife* needed to be alone today, but I didn't see it. My *wife* asked to be alone today, and I took over some of *her* work—but I begrudged *her* the gift.

Forgive me especially for ignoring your blessed commandment to withdraw and rest. I've put work ahead of rest. I've put my activities ahead of your wisdom (Neh. 13:15-22).

Fᴏʀɢɪᴠᴇ ᴍᴇ. Change me. Make me like you:

Help me to realize that it is for my *wife*'s health that *she* withdraw: *her* spiritual health, *her* emotional health, *her* physical health. Therefore it serves our marriage after all. Give me the wisdom and the willingness to support *her* sabbath time apart.

Let me take an example from *her* and also seek a prayerful solitude, a Sabbath rest, for my health and for our family (Isa. 58:13-14).

O Creator of the seventh day, the Sabbath day, that day of necessary rest, re-create in our marriage such a rest time as a regular ritual that we share together.

WW

THANKSGIVING FOR MY SPOUSE'S TALENTS

Read the assigned lines with one another. Then switch roles and read the prayer again, thinking of your partner in new and thankful ways.

WIFE AND HUSBAND: Dear Giver of all that is good in us, thank you for the many talents and gifts that you have given my spouse:

WIFE: For strong hands that build and repair;

HUSBAND: For a sense of frugality and the brains to handle finances;

WIFE: For a green thumb that shares in your creation;

HUSBAND: For the milk and the love that nourish our children;

WIFE: For a creative mind;

HUSBAND: For the care with which she grooms herself and keeps her body strong and healthy; she'll live at least as long as I do;

WIFE: For a kind heart that knows and fills the needs of others;

HUSBAND: For her accuracy of thought, her ability to organize our complex lives;

WIFE: For a humility that sees all others as worthy of attention;

HUSBAND: For desserts;

WIFE: For a generosity that knows no bounds;

HUSBAND: For her love of Scriptures, her unquenchable thirst to study them;

WIFE: For gentle ears that patiently listen;

HUSBAND: For her peaceful obedience to God, her pursuit of goodness and morality;

WIFE: For an encouraging spirit that uplifts the sorrowing;

HUSBAND: For her ability to pray, powerfully, persistently;

WIFE: For faithfulness to you;

HUSBAND: For common sense when I am troubled, emotional, given to wild exaggerations;

WIFE: For honesty in all things;

HUSBAND: For her perfect choices in giving gifts to others, and the insight that understands the hearts of others;

WIFE AND HUSBAND: Thank you that my spouse has chosen to use these gifts for the glory of your name and for the good of your kingdom. Teach me to appreciate these gifts, to tend and encourage them, and to honor them as evidence of your dwelling in *his/her* heart. Amen.

RW and WW

PRAYERS

LOVE AND LOVING

COMPANIONSHIP AFTER YEARS OF MARRIAGE

GOD OF LOVE, you gave Adam and Eve to each other to be companions one for the other. Thank you for the companion you gave to me—the one who accompanies me in joy and in sorrow, in peaceful times and in turbulent times, in health and in illness, in riches and in poverty.

Thank you for being the Fountainhead of all that is good in our marriage and the Healer of all that is not. Be our companion for the rest of our marriage journey, until the end when one of us lays the other to rest in your loving arms. In Jesus' name.
Amen.

RW

O Lord of every covenant, what gifts you have given us through the years of our life's covenant, our marriage:

In the beginning of our life together, you grant us a passionate love.

When survival becomes our primary concern, you make us partners, two different people with different sets of skills celebrating the differences by becoming one complete whole, working together, raising children together, trusting one another.

In middle age, when we are home alone again, you bless us with the freedom to rediscover one another, the pure pleasure of being together, the comfort of a long trust, the consolation of one completely perfect friend, the kindness of sexuality when all the pressures are past.

In old age we discover that you have been saving us one for the other, since now we take turns nursing each other, feeding sweetly on memories together, delighting in the generations that come after us and who carry on the expressions of your love.

O God, what strength and hope it is, that we both believe in you, for we will not be separated in death—no, not even in death.

WW

LOVEMAKING

O CREATOR, WHAT A WONDER!

You made us not merely spirit; you made us as bodies too!

When we live at peace with you, then we may be naked with one another and not ashamed (Gen. 2:25). It is our sins against you that cause us to cover up before each other (Gen. 3:6-9). Your forgiveness is our freedom: to love each other; to love our bodies; to make love with our bodies!

Thank you, Lord. This gift is delightful. I love the touch and the flesh of my *wife*. It causes in my flesh sensations and physical responses I could never know alone, sweetness sweeter than I have words to say.

But keep me, Lord, from taking my pleasure only. Teach me to learn and to accomplish the pleasure of my *wife*. Give *her* the words and me the ears. Let it be genuine love in me that reaches to *her*.

And as we grow older, Lord, and as our bodies change with age, let no shame disturb the relationship. Still let the touch and the joining of our flesh grant solace one to the other, and love, and a blessed satisfaction.

Praise to you, Creator, and to you, O Word Made Flesh: for you make sacred the love we express for one another in and by the flesh.

WW

THANKSGIVING FOR LOVE

DEAR FATHER, from whom all love comes, you love us with a love that is never exhausted.

Because you are the source of our love for each other, you help me to love when I cannot. You help my *husband* to love me when *he* cannot. Thank you for the times *he* has loved me when I haven't been very lovable. Thank you for the times *he* has loved me by sacrificing *his* own desires and needs. Thank you for the times *he* loved me enough to forgive me. Thank you for the times *he* loved me even when I was angry or depressed or grieving. Thank you for the love that I know can come only from you.

Fill me with your love so that when my love isn't enough, I can love well through you. In Jesus' name. Amen.

RW

TEMPTATIONS TO BE UNFAITHFUL

LORD GOD, before witnesses and under your gaze, I promised my *wife* that I would be faithful only unto *her* as long as we both shall live.

Wherever I go, my ring is a sign that *she* (and my promise to *her*) goes with me.

Whoever I meet, they cannot know the whole of me if they do not know my marriage. My full person includes my *wife*; it is shaped by *her* character, and all I do affects *her* too.

When temptation comes, O Lord, make me immediately alert to it—that it is a temptation to sin, to break my promise, to act as if there was no marriage and I had no *wife*.

When temptation comes, O Lord, keep me from thinking only of myself, my own desires. Keep me from justifying a sin, as if I somehow deserved a satisfaction that ignores my *wife*. Keep me from finding fault with my *wife* in order to excuse my sin—as if *she* deserved punishment.

When temptation comes, O Lord, be with me. Empower me to respond as you responded to the devil in the wilderness (Matt. 4:1-11)—with the Word of God, with faith, with your strength. Teach me to use your name: "Begone, Satan! In the name of Jesus Christ, I rebuke you: leave me and my marriage alone!"

When temptation comes, O Lord, help me carry it to my *wife*. Be with us when we discuss it. Let the sharing of knowledge and our relationship (and the truth uttered in faith together) strengthen us both against the tempter and keep us each from sinning.

Surround us with your angels, ministering unto us and our marriage as they ministered to you in the wilderness.

We are yours, Jesus. We belong to you. Preserve us, O Lord, for in you we take refuge.

WW

TEMPTATIONS TO ESCAPE

DEAR JESUS, when you walked among us, you were tempted in the same ways we are tempted. You understand our struggle. Because you were tempted and resisted, we know that we can draw on your power to help us resist the sins that grip us.

I confess my weakness, Lord, when I am tempted to use alcohol or drugs to ease the stresses in my day. Instead of facing problems and working toward solutions, I tend to run away and hide. Rather than talking through a difficulty with my *husband*, I want to drink or take pills to escape. Instead of turning to you, I am tempted to turn to alcohol or drugs. Forgive my weakness, Lord. Forgive me when my fears are greater than my trust in you. Forgive me when I choose alcohol or drugs over my *husband.*

You are greater than any temptation that threatens our marriage, Lord. Give me your power to withstand the temptation to use alcohol or drugs in inappropriate and dangerous ways. And if I find their enticements too strong, give me the strength to seek out those who can help me become and stay strong. In your name I plead. Amen.

RW

PROTECTION FROM ASSAULTS ON MARRIAGE

DEAR GOD, OUR GREAT PROTECTOR,

We live in a world full of sin and evil. Some evil attacks from without, but some resides within. Save us from the assaults of Satan that threaten our marriage. Save us from gossip or criticism from family or friends, from interfering parents and in-laws. Save us from the pressures of stressful jobs, rebellious children, and financial difficulties. Save us from the deficiencies of weariness, fear, and discouragement.

You know these dangers, Lord, and you know how fragile marriages can be. Be our Strength and our Protector. Preserve our union and save us from all things that threaten our commitment to each other. Make our love strong and keep our hearts loving each other as you have loved us. Amen.

RW

LIFE'S CHANGES

Lᴏʀᴅ, this is a perilous time for us. Our relationship is under unusual stress—exactly when we need each other, and must trust each other, the most. Savior, save us now.

As you appeared to Jacob at Bethel (Gen. 28:10-22), make your presence known to both of us, even in these new circumstances; for you are everywhere, and though the whole world might change, you do not.

O Word of God, keep the communications clear, open, and honest between my *wife* and me.

When one of us needs the greater care, grant the other the greater strength.

When the storm of change lasts so long that it threatens to capsize us, our marriage, our mutual trust, our peace of mind, then stand up in the ship of our household and speak your powerful command: "Peace! Be still!" Also, do for us what you did for the disciples, caution us for our fear and weak faith and cause us to wonder again at your divine authority (Mark 4:35-41).

You are with us. You are in each of us for the other. You are between us in our marriage. You are our Lord and our life and our love. We give all our uncertainties to you.

Whether together or apart, let both spouses read Psalm 46 over and over again.

WW

AGING

Dear God who spans all time and all space,

Thank you for the life you have given us in this time and place. As we move from birth to death on this earth, walk with us. As circumstances in our lives change, be our stability.

You were constant as we adjusted to being married. You were steadfast during the years of raising children. You stayed with us as we adjusted to our empty nest.

Remain with us now, Lord, as we come to the later years of our lives. Be our faithful companion as our bodies change and cease to function as well as they used to. We've put on weight, our blood pressures have risen, our energy levels have decreased, and we ache from arthritis. Menopause and impotence affect our intimacy. And sometimes we don't feel very lovable.

Remind us, Lord, that in spite of all that, you have given us each other—a husband who loves even the bumps and wrinkles on his wife's body; a wife who is filled with tenderness for her husband's thicker waist and thinner hair. And when we get discouraged, remind us that each day brings us closer to the fullness of life with you in eternity where perfection will be ours. Amen.

RW

WHEN LOVE FEELS NEW

GOD OF ETERNAL HOPE,

You continually surprise us with your blessings.

When we were first married, our love was new and exciting. We looked forward to being together at the end of the day. We enjoyed going out to dinner together. We took pleasure in sharing evenings with friends. We treasured long walks in the summer and ice skating in the winter. We loved making our tiny apartment into a home. Thank you for all of those blessings and joys of the newly married.

Now we thank you also for the blessings and joys that flow from a mature love that still feels fresh and exciting.

HUSBAND: Since our nest has been emptied of children, I've begun both to rediscover the woman I married long ago and to discover a new, more mature peace and wisdom in her. Thank you for that something unshakable after all the changes of these years.

WIFE: Thank you for a husband who still brings flowers and writes poetry.

HUSBAND: Thank you for a wife who touches me at odd moments, spontaneously kisses me, offers unexpected words of praise—and fills my common day with bright flashes of delight.

WIFE: Thank you for a husband who still enjoys a dinner out or an evening with friends; for a friend who loves a summer sunset and a walk in the winter's first snow.

HUSBAND: Thank you for a wife who lingers at the table when we eat supper alone, talking, taking a genuine interest in the things that interest me.

WIFE: Thank you for a husband who plays Scrabble by the fire.

HUSBAND: Thank you for a marriage in which we both can peacefully—with a glad good humor—watch our bodies change with age, a droop here, a bulge there, but never the sense of loss or embarrassment. We share each blotch and spot, and neither one of us ages alone.

TOGETHER: For keeping our love fresh even as it deepens and matures, I thank you, God. Amen.

RW and WW

GIFTS

Dᴇᴀʀ Gᴏᴅ, you saw ahead from the beginning of time the blessing of mates well suited to each other. Thank you for your wise and generous gift to me—my *husband*. And thank you for the gifts that come to me through *him:*

~ time away when I need it;
~ tender care when I am ill;
~ well-chosen gifts when I don't expect them;
~ birthday celebrations when I feel old;
~ chocolate candy bars when I feel low;
~ dinners out when I'm too tired to cook;
~ visits to friends or relatives, even when *he's* tired;
~ time alone with each other;
~ massaging my feet at the end of a long day;
~ calling to tell me *he* loves me when *he's* away.

For all these things, and for my *husband* by whom they come, I thank you. Amen.

RW

WHEN WE ARE FIGHTING

Lord God, we are weak. We need your strength and mercy. We can't make peace on our own.

I am dividing us, my *wife* and me. It doesn't matter who started the fight or what we're fighting about. I'm focusing on *her* fault and my innocence. I think about vengeance, Lord. I want *her* to suffer as much as I have. No, more than I have. I want to make *her* feel guilty. I can't speak one good word to *her*. So I keep my mouth shut and feel righteous about it.

But in these things, O God, I'm a sinner; I like my anger; therefore I make peace impossible.

Even though it will cause me the new hurt of a burning and purging condemnation, come Lord Jesus!

Let me focus on you. (Read Luke 23:33-49, then reread, aloud, verses 34, 40-43, 46-47.) You died to take away from me both the sins and all their consequences. Forgive me now, Jesus.

With your powerful mercy, wipe out my anger. Give me, as you gave Solomon, a "listening heart," so that I might know what is truly behind my *wife*'s hurt and anger.

Jesus, you healed and forgave the paralyzed man whose friends brought him to you (Mark 2: 1-12). Even so, forgive us and heal our marriage; heal the wounds we've given one another. Let our healing be a sign of your presence and forgiveness; and let it strengthen us in the future.

And since we cannot on our own, please, O Father, give us peace.

WW

ARGUMENTS AND DISAGREEMENTS

Dear God of reconciliation, Healer of discord and strife,

You have provided a way to heal the hurt and anger that sometimes disrupts our marriage. When our fallen nature allows arguments and disagreements to come between us and unsettle this union, you make it possible for us freely to confess our sin to the other and to be generous in our forgiving. Take away the sinful desire to hurt the one I love. Remove from my heart pride and the need to be right. Forgive my carelessness in the words I choose when we argue. Cleanse me from bitterness and the fear of not being loved. Let my discourse be free from rancor and the desire to punish. Forgive me for my anger when we argue or disagree, and guard me from sin. Keep me from dredging up the past and reviving what has already been confessed and forgiven.

Through your generous grace and forgiveness, direct my ways and keep me pure, even as we disagree. Turn both of our hearts and minds toward you so that all we do—even our disagreements—may be pleasing to you. I pray in the name of Jesus, my Forgiver and Guide. Amen.

RW

Jᴇsᴜs, I ᴄᴏɴꜰᴇss:

I know how to wound my *wife* with words, crushing *her* self-confidence to elevate myself.

I know how to fight *her* with silence; when I'm angry or depressed, I make *her* pay for it.

We argue, sometimes, not because I'm right but because I hate to be wrong; I want to win.

Sometimes I force an argument in order to justify my own desires: self-righteously to storm out of the house; sweetly to sink in self-pity.

Rather than listening, I wait for my turn to talk.

I exaggerate, saying, "You always . . ." and "You never . . ." when in fact the argument is seldom *her* fault and never more *her* fault than mine.

Jesus, forgive me; change me; fill me with your Holy Spirit (John 20:22).

Whatever the topic of discussion, let my goal be truly to comfort my *wife*.

Let me always speak the truth, glorifying not me, but you (John 16:13-14).

Let my manner and my language bear witness, Jesus, to you.

Let the character and the source of my every discussion with my *wife* be the fruits of the Spirit: love, joy, peace, patience, kindness, goodness, faithfulness, gentleness, self-control (Gal. 5:22-23).

WW

A PRIVATE RITE—CONFESSION AND FORGIVENESS

We suggest that first each spouse—the one who sinned and the one who received the sin—privately pray the prayers that follow. Then engage in the rite of confession and forgiveness together, aloud.

Note: If the sin and the act of forgiveness are too great to handle alone, please turn to a pastor or to trusted friends who can, without blame or disgust or taking sides, participate as loving and faithful leaders in the confession and the word of forgiveness.

Prayers

GOD OF MERCY, your forgiveness is forever available to those who seek it.

I need your forgiveness. I hurt my *husband* because I was thinking only of myself and not of *him*. My carelessness of *his* feelings, insensitivity to *his* needs, and my self-absorption have caused me to sin against *him* and bring a rift between us. Forgive my selfishness and lack of care. My sin against my *husband* is also a sin against you, and I need your forgiveness. I humble myself before you and beg your forgiveness. Help me also to humble myself before my *husband* and confess my sin. Your grace is full and your mercy is boundless. Renew our relationship and turn our hearts to you as the Source of the love between us. Make us whole again, through the love of your Son Jesus. Amen.

RW

LORD JESUS, my *wife* wounded me so deeply that I still feel the pain. *She* has sinned against me.

She has also repented of the sin, and now asks (if only indirectly, by signals, gestures, expressions) for my forgiveness.

Therefore I turn to you.

I know how weak and sullied is my own human forgiveness. I confess that I want *her* to be humbled, to suffer a remorse equal to my hurt. I find in myself the desire for "getting even."

Therefore I turn to you.

I need your forgiveness first, so that I don't compound the sin. I remember how much I've sinned against you—infinitely more than my *wife* could ever sin against me. I remember and rejoice in the infinite measure of your forgiveness for me. I beg that that forgiveness flow through me to my *wife*.

And then shall my forgiveness be pure and true. And then shall our marital relationship heal well and truly. And then shall you take up a genuine residence in our marriage.

WW

A Private Rite of Confession and Forgiveness

1. Don't act unilaterally or spontaneously. Choose together a specific place and time for this act.
2. Begin by reading aloud 1 John 1:5 through 2:6.

   Know that each of you has been cleansed of all sin by the blood of Jesus, the Son of God. Know that in that forgiveness you may have "fellowship with one another." But note the need of confession. It is a sacred act, whereby you may both hear and feel the genuine forgiveness God has prepared for you.

3. Let the one confessing read aloud Psalm 32:1-5.
4. Let the one through whom God is sending forgiveness read aloud Luke 6:37-38 and James 5:16-18.
5. In simple words, without any effort to justify or explain, let the one confessing now describe the sin. Speak, too, words of true repentance and hunger for forgiveness.
6. Now let the one through whom forgiveness comes, in simple words, assure the one confessing that Jesus has forgiven and that, by the love and grace of Jesus, so do you forgive.

7. Together pray the Lord's Prayer.

8. Let some sign or token of forgiveness be given: it may be as humble as a hug; it may be some small gift that the forgiving one had gotten in advance, according to your own character and relationship.

9. Let the one forgiven *now* (in the strength and grace of that forgiveness) make a specific pledge not to repeat the sin, and offer some sign of the pledge—such as an act that might become habitual, an act that protects against sinful repetition.

10. Allow this time to last as long as it seems good, even if the two of you sit in silence a while, quietly communing with the Holy Spirit now present.

11. Eat something together. Drink something.

WW

PRAYERS
TIMES OF SUFFERING

WHEN MY SPOUSE IS SICK OR INJURED

First read Matthew 8:1-17. Then pray . . .

LORD JESUS, HEALER OF EVERY DISEASE, HEAL MY *WIFE*.

Jesus, compassionate for the weak, strengthen my *wife*. You, Lord, who healed the Centurion's servant without going to his house, even from heaven heal my *wife*. Increase my faith in you, my trust in your love and your watchful power.

You, Jesus, who healed leprosy with a touch, use the touch of medical healers to heal my *wife*.

You, Lord Jesus Christ, who cast out the unclean spirits with a word, use my words—my poor words, my clumsy words, my dearly loving words—to ease the internal torment of my *wife*.

Keep me from failings and fears. I promised to keep my *wife* both in sickness and in health; therefore, Lord, keep me from self-pity and personal irritation. Teach me to pray out loud beside *her* for *her* comfort and trust.

Jesus, Jesus, heal my *wife:* through me, through the Spirit, by your abiding love, bring *her* to health again. Amen.

WW

WHEN I AM SICK OR INJURED

DEAR JESUS, GREAT PHYSICIAN, when you walked this earth many years ago, you healed those who were sick and in need of your gentle touch. I pray today for your mercy and healing as I struggle with this illness (injury). My body hurts and I feel so weak and discouraged. I plead for your healing for both my body and my spirit. When I hurt, ease my pain. When my spirit weakens, renew my strength.

Bless those who care for me during this time: doctors and nurses whose compassionate hands work skillfully and tirelessly to minister to my physical needs; my pastor (priest) who feeds my soul; my *husband* and children whose patience and love comfort me and give me strength; my family and friends who tirelessly carry the extra burdens my illness (injury) has caused; and all others who quietly minister to me and my *husband*.

In the end, Lord, if you choose not to remove this suffering, teach me how to bear it. Draw me close to you and remind me that you willingly suffered for my sake.

Please also give my *husband* the strength to cope. Increase our love for one another and strengthen our faith. Relieve our fears and give us hope. Remind us that when we wake and when we sleep, you are there, always ready to hear and heal. Amen.

RW

WHEN MY SPOUSE IS DEPRESSED OR DISTRESSED

O LORD JESUS CHRIST, how much I love my *wife!* Oh, how I yearn for *her* healing! But how weak and helpless I feel. Yet you have chosen the weak and foolish through whom to work.

So I begin here, bowing down in prayer before you, believing in your promise that whenever we pray in your name, the Father will give us our deepest need (John 15:16; 16:23-24).

Come, place your hand on my *wife.* Heal *her* as you healed so many who called upon you when you walked the earth, healed their bodies and their spirits.

Come. Choose me through whom to work your wonders:

~ fill me with your wisdom, that I learn what to do and what not to do for *her;*
~ fill me with your strength, that I be enabled to do it;
~ fill me with your patience, that I might endure as long as necessary and not grow weary;
~ fill me with your loving-kindness, that I give my help freely and ungrudgingly;
~ send me wise people in whom to confide, from whom to learn skills and medicines; and grant my labors success.

Continue by reading Psalm 118:1-18. Pray it both for yourself and for your spouse.

WW

WHEN MY SPOUSE IS EXHAUSTED OR TROUBLED

Read 2 Corinthians 1:3-4. Then pray . . .

JESUS, give me eyes to see:
    when my dear one is exhausted and troubled.
Jesus, give me the heart to know:
    that then it is my marital responsibility to comfort and restore *her.*
Jesus, give me the wisdom to choose:
    the best means for comfort and restoration, never forcing my own ideas, ever
    searching *her* face and mind and condition for the true need and the best medicine.
Jesus, give me the patience:
    that I might serve willingly and faithfully as long as *she* has the need.
Jesus, give me joy and faith:
    that I might be a witness, a visible connection between *her* and you;
    that I never cease to pray for *her.*

WW

BEFORE DIAGNOSIS OR SURGERY

First read Psalm 18, verses 1-6, 16-19, 31-36, 49-50. Then pray . . .

LORD, WE DON'T KNOW THE FUTURE. We can't tell what's going to happen tomorrow. We stand at the edge of a terrible darkness, about to enter there—and we're frightened.

Suddenly the life we have been living so thoughtlessly seems painfully sweet and good—and vulnerable. What if we lose it? What if it changes? Will sickness or surgery now reduce our familiar life? Or ruin it altogether?

Be with us, O Lord, our strength. O Lord God, be our rock and fortress, our strong deliverer.

We know in our minds that the darkness is never dark to you, that you know our futures because you already dwell there, waiting for us to arrive.

But now we beg you to teach our hearts and souls to believe in your presence. Give us trust. Give us faith. Give us peace again, Lord God.

For Jesus Christ, your Son, went into a darkness more dismal than any other; he suffered the extreme of sickness; he died; he rose glorious from death—and now he walks with us into our trial and darkness. We do not go alone.

When we lie down under the doctor's hand tomorrow, O Lord, let us cling to your hand.

Make our hearts still, knowing that you are God. Amen.

WW

DIFFICULTY AT WORK

GOD OF COMFORT, I had a hard day at work today. Nothing seemed to go right, and there was friction with my coworkers. Forgive my resentments and frustrations that contributed to the tension. Give me a forgiving and generous spirit so that my desire is to heal and not hurt, to encourage and not discourage, to build up and not tear down, to be graceful and not judgmental, to listen and not jump to conclusions, to make peace and not disharmony.

I need your comfort and strength, Lord. Remind me that you are present during these troubling times at work. Come now also to keep me from infecting my home with the tensions from work. Remind me that my *husband* has stresses in *his* day as well. Thank you for a *husband* who is willing to share my burden; give me the grace to receive *his* encouragement. Make our home a safe haven from all that causes us distress, but at the same time, a place where burdens may be shared. Amen.

RW

LOSS OF JOB

Lᴏʀᴅ, I'ᴠᴇ ʟᴏsᴛ ᴍʏ ᴊᴏʙ, ᴀɴᴅ I'ᴍ sᴏ ᴀғʀᴀɪᴅ.

I'm struggling with feelings of anger and resentment over how I was let go. I'm feeling humiliated and worthless. I'm terrified about what the future holds. My family depends on me, and I feel like I've let them down. I'm discouraged because I don't have another job.

Forgive me, Lord, for my fears. Teach me how to trust you. My faith has never been tested like it is now. Strengthen me and make my faith strong. Keep me from taking my anger out on my *husband* by helping me remember that *he* is also fearful about the future. Keep me from withdrawing inside myself. Remind me that my worth comes from you, not from a job. Increase my faith and give me your peace. Guide my future and keep me from sin.

Hold me, comfort me, bless me.

Hold my *husband,* comfort *him,* bless *him.*

Hold us both in your loving arms.

Amen.

RW

WHEN MY SPOUSE LOSES A JOB

Read Hebrews 13:5,6. Then pray . . .

Lord, I confess:
In my moments of fear and hopelessness, I blame my *wife* for the loss.
In my confusion, I withdraw and feel that *I* have been wronged.
I forget you, neglect you and your love and faithfulness.
I've been blind to the deeper losses of my *wife:* self-respect; personhood; an acceptable identity in society; a sense of value even before me and the family, feeling unworthy even of my love.

Forgive me, Lord. Change me. Use me (as once I promised to be faithful to my *wife* through all conditions of life) as an instrument for personal healing, for hope and renewal:
that together we take a realistic view of the situation;
that neither of us ever feels alone or separate from the other;
that I speak the truth, powerfully, of my *wife*'s worth and character:
that we pray together; and that we trust your providence and your promise never to leave us;
and that when we experience a true revival—new life and identity arising from this sorrow—we remember to give all thanks and praise to you. Amen.

WW

PRAYERS
FOR THE FAITH OF MY SPOUSE

WHEN FAITH IS STRONG

Lord God, thank you! With all my heart I give you thanks because you have given me a *wife* whose spirit is as strong as the cedars of Lebanon.

She is a Deborah, who never doubts your presence and strength, even when under attack (Judg. 4). With *her* I am protected as if in a fortress.

She is Isaiah, who sees your coming and your love even when I feel blind and broken and shut away in exile (Isa. 40:1-11).

My *wife* is my spiritual companion whose obedience and faithfulness to you strengthens my own faith and obedience. I rejoice that we serve you together, for together our discipleship is whole and our praise is doubled. Amen.

WW

WHEN FAITH IS WEAK OR COLD OR ABSENT

JESUS, I believe in you. I believe in your love for everyone. I believe that you "desire all people to be saved and to come to the knowledge of the truth," and I believe that you are the Savior, the one who has already accomplished that salvation, the one who mediates always between us and God (1 Tim. 2:4-6).

Now, under the banner of those truths and promises, I pray for my *wife*. I pray with all my heart. I pray with true humility, knowing that I cannot, but that you can (and you want to) plant a strong faith in *her* soul. I love *her*, Jesus. And I trust you. Please, please, show *her* your face. Draw *her* soul and mind to you. By your Holy Spirit, fill *her* with a hunger for holiness that can only be fulfilled by you—and then come, fill *her* with your Spirit and the joy of your salvation.

I am Jairus, beseeching you for the life of my *wife*: "Come and lay your hands on *her* that *she* may be made well, and live" (Mark 5:21-24, 35-43). You are the same Jesus who gave that child life. Do it again, spiritually, for my *wife*.

I am—yes, and sometimes I feel like—the widow who kept begging the judge till he gave her what she wanted (Luke 18:1-8). I will keep beseeching you, Lord, for the sake of my *wife,* until you answer and fill *her* with faith and love for you.

WW

PRAYERS

ROLES AS CHILDREN AND PARENTS

PARENTING TOGETHER

LORD, sometimes I feel overwhelmed with parenthood.

I'm constantly tired because my life seems to be controlled by everyone but myself. It's a strain to be "on duty" twenty-four hours a day, seven days a week. How often the most carefully made plans have to be altered or abandoned because one of the children is ill or needs last-minute help with a school project. It's hard to find time for myself or my *husband*.

Sometimes, Lord, I feel so alone in this holy work. Sometimes it makes me angry that I am the one who drives them to and from band rehearsals and basketball practice, helps them with their homework, and cares for them when they are ill.

Forgive my resentments, Lord, and remind me that my children have been placed into this marriage by a loving God. Forgive me for assuming that my *husband* doesn't want to share the responsibility. Forgive me for rushing to blame rather than taking time to work out a plan for both of us to parent in ways that strengthen both the family and the marriage. Keep me from self-centeredness and self-pity. Let my goal always be to glorify you and nourish the family. Let my motives always be to strengthen the family so that each child knows love and care from both parents and has the security of parents that love and care for each other. Work within us, Lord—in me and in my *husband*—so that we live in gratitude for the privilege of caring for the children you gave us. Amen.

RW

LORD, I CONFESS:

I have too often felt that the job of parenting was more my *wife*'s than mine.

I used my natural ignorance about babies to excuse me from a balanced share in washing, feeding, dressing, comforting them.

I did not support *her* schedules of child and family activities, of necessary discipline.

When *she* complained about *her* life with the children, I turned a deaf ear. I considered it a failing in *her,* and privately blamed *her* for it. I didn't sit down to discuss a division of this labor.

Father, you established marriage for children, thereby giving every child two parents. Forgive me for neglecting your will. Change me. Grant me your wisdom.

Help me to open time in my every day, both for the children, and for my *wife* alone.

When *she* can no longer handle a particular child at a particular time, teach me to see *her* need; empower me to take the responsibility upon myself; grant my parental work wisdom, patience, and a blessed effect for the child and for the family.

I am a *father* and a *husband.* Let my two roles, O God, each balance and serve the other.

Without you I am foolish; I stumble. With you I am strong, stable, wise in discipline and in love.

WW

THE GOODNESS OF PARENTS-IN-LAW

O LORD OF NATIONS AND TRIBES AND FAMILIES, protector of the generations, what a gift you created and preserved for me in the bosom of another household!

Thank you for my *wife*.

Thank you for the unique intermingling of characteristics that *she* received from *her* parents, from their love together.

Thank you for providing *her* childhood and youth with shelter and nourishment through the service of *her* parents.

Thank you for the shaping and training that *her* mother and father accomplished in *her*.

I see their wisdom, their talents, their skills and decisions in *her*. Endowing *her*, they have enriched my life as well. And they have received me!

When I married, O Lord, you granted me a new source of love and support in my parents-in-law.

Read the book of Ruth for a beautiful portrayal of the love of in-laws for one another—concluding in a marriage. The promise of God is preserved in such families, since King David came through their seed, and through David came the Christ.

WW

THANKSGIVING FOR GOOD PARENTS

DEAR GOD AND FATHER, you are the perfect parent to us and the model of parental love to all your children. I thank you for the blessings I have received from my parents:

~ for love and nurture and encouragement;
~ for faithfulness to you and peace in the face of adversity;
~ for joy in their children and grandchildren;
~ for lessons in tithing and sharing;
~ for generosity and wholeness of spirit;
~ for love of the unlovely;
~ for love and honor of each other.

Help me to live in the good ways they taught me, especially in my marriage and family. I thank you for parents that continue to support us and encourage us. Help me to draw on their example to be a good *wife* and a good parent. I thank you also that you are my Father. Without you as the head of our household, without your Son's redemption of our failures, and without your Spirit's comfort and breath, I could not love well. Thank you for parenting both me and my family. Amen.

RW

PARENTS VERSUS SPOUSE

Therefore man leaves his father and his mother and cleaves to his wife, and they become one flesh (Gen. 2:24).

ALMIGHTY GOD, you created marriage as the most intimate relationship between a man and a woman. In order to keep that intimacy sacred and healthy, you asked that it be the primary relationship in the lives of a husband and a wife.

When I was a child, my relationship with my parents was primary.

But when I married, you asked me to leave my parents in order to cleave to my *wife*.

I confess, Lord, that I haven't always left my parental past behind me; sometimes allowing the influence of my parents to displace the rights, the needs, and the wishes of my *wife*; sometimes letting the sins that my parents committed against me in my childhood to affect my moods and my behaviors in our marriage; sometimes repeating their sins, but now against my own family; sometimes nursing an old anger for the wounds of my past.

Creator, make me new. Liberate me from the mistakes and sins of my parents, that I neither remember them in anger nor repeat them in my family. Help me in my marriage not to mimic the failures of humankind, but rather to image your love and wisdom, O my Holy Father. Amen.

WW

MERCY FOR DIFFICULT PARENTS

Dear Father, you put us into families so that we can be nurtured and cared for. But sometimes our parents burden us with baggage from our childhoods. Help me to put away the bad effects of their criticism and shame, anger and indiscriminate punishment, meanness of spirit, emotional degradation.

Sometimes my parents interfere with our family. Help me to forgive when they criticize how we raise our children or cause friction between us by criticizing one or both of us. Help me to forgive when they gossip about us to our brothers and sisters or when they don't love my *husband* or our children. Help me to forgive when they get angry with us for not fulfilling their expectations or make us feel guilty for not visiting enough.

Remind me, Father, that I am not perfect either. I, too, have sinned against my children. Rather than dwelling on my parents' sins, show me how not to repeat their sins with my own children. I've also sinned against my *husband*. Show me how to keep us close in spite of sinful patterns learned in childhood. Forgive my parents their past weaknesses and restore both them and me to wholeness. You are my perfect Father who sent my brother Jesus to redeem my parents and me. Thank you. Amen.

RW

CARING FOR AGED PARENTS

GOD OF ALL ETERNITY, thank you for the care you have shown me through my parents—for their love and sacrifice and for staying the course with me even through the difficult times.

Now they are old, Lord, and they need my care. Give me wisdom to know how best to honor and serve them. Keep me from feeling that they interrupt my life when they need my companionship and help. Help me to increase their joy and peace in these latter days of their lives.

Give me patience to listen with joy to the stories I've heard before, just as they listened to mine during my childhood. Give me the willingness to cut their toenails and wash their hair. Give me energy to stay in touch.

And as my responsibilities increase, don't let me forget that I also have a *husband* who needs my care. Help me to balance the needs of my parents with the needs of my *husband*, as well as my own spiritual and physical needs.

When I am neglectful, forgive me. When I am tired, refresh me. When I am discouraged, strengthen me. Embrace us all, Father, with your strong and loving arms. Amen.

RW

WHEN MY SPOUSE IS CARING FOR AGED PARENTS

LORD GOD, they are my parents too. Their weakness and their needs, which now burden my *wife*, are my burdens too. But it is not the same thing, after all.

My *wife*'s heart is more affected by their struggles than mine; *her* real work and emotional life are more exhausted than mine, because they are *her* obligation more than they are mine.

Therefore, I pray for *her* strength—that you, O Lord, would be *her* strength. Give *her* restful nights. Ease *her* days here at home to allow *her* a true attention with *her* parents.

I pray for *her* heart—that no guilt or grief should enter there, but only your love so that *her* love for *her* parents remains pure and limitless.

I pray for myself—that I might be alert to my *wife*'s needs and weaknesses while serving others; that I might be a strong, abiding support; that I might love *her* with your love, until we make a circle of sacred love and holy service together, in which you are the center.

All we do, dear Lord, we do with you, for you, and under your care.

WW

SPOUSES FOR OUR CHILDREN

DEAR GREAT PROVIDER, you give us what we need to live our lives under your love.

You have provided me with a *husband* who is faithful to you and loves me more than *himself*. You have given me children who love you. As they grow, Father, teach them how to be good husbands and wives. And when they are ready, bring them together with a suitable spouse. Prepare their future spouses now and teach them your ways. Train their hearts to be faithful to you so that they, together with our children, can encourage one another in faith.

Give our children wisdom to seek your guidance as they choose their life partners. And direct them to the ones you have prepared for them. You hold the future of our children. Hold also the future of those whom you have chosen for them as their futures become one together. In Jesus' name. Amen.

RW

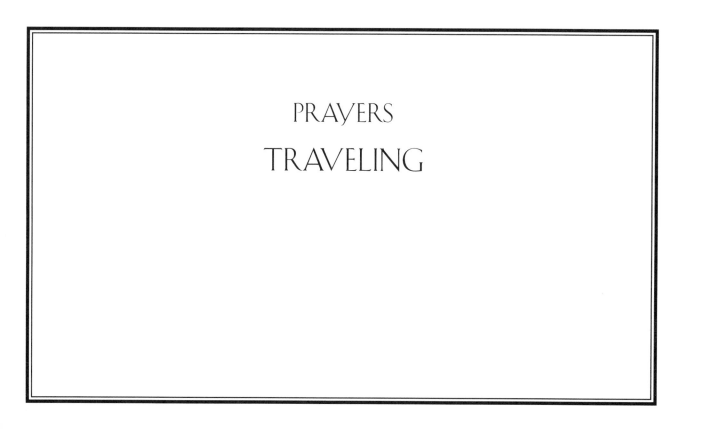

PRAYERS

TRAVELING

BEFORE A TRIP TAKEN TOGETHER

ALMIGHTY GOD, wherever we go, whenever we get there, you are already there ahead of us. However we travel, whatever the road, you pace the way beside us.

Where can we go from your Spirit? If we ascend to heaven, you are there. If we lie down in Sheol, you are there.

If we take the wings of the morning and dwell in the uttermost parts of the sea, even there your hand shall lead us, and your right hand shall hold us (Ps. 139:7-12).

Go with us now.

Keep us safe from danger as we go.

Grant us confidence when we arrive.

We trust, O Lord, in your steadfast faithfulness, for you yourself have promised us: "Mountains may depart and the hills be removed, but my steadfast love shall not depart from you" (Isa. 54:10).

So be it with us now. Amen.

WW

HOME AGAIN

O GIVE THANKS TO THE LORD, for he is good, and his mercy endures forever.

You are our God. We owe you our hearts' thanksgiving. You are our God. We will extol you forever. You are our God; we are your people, and that is the wholeness of any family.

Home again! Whole again! We are at peace.

O give thanks to the Lord, for he is good, and his mercy endures forever. Amen.

WW

BEFORE A TRIP ONE SPOUSE WILL TAKE
Spoken by the one who waits at home.

First, for a powerful picture of God's help for those on difficult journeys, read Psalm 107:1-3 and 23-32. Whether your spouse is in danger—physical, financial, moral, or psychological danger—God calms the seas and sees her *through. Then pray:*

O LORD OUR GOD, watch over my *wife* as *she* travels. You, as a pillar of cloud and light, led Israel through the wilderness, protecting them and bringing them finally to their home. Keep, protect, and bring my dear one home as well.

Let neither danger nor temptation overcome *her*. Keep *her* soul, heart, and body both safe and pure. Carry my love to *her*. Assure *her* of my abiding love.

And carry *her* home. We are a family bound closely together, whatever the space between us. We are your family, Lord. Your Spirit is our binding. Amen.

WW

BEFORE A TRIP ONE SPOUSE WILL TAKE
Spoken by both.

The previous prayer may be prayed for the traveling spouse—before the trip—by the one staying home, only changing the referents and pronouns where italicized. Then let each in turn face the other, place hands on his shoulders, and say:

Angels before you.
Angels behind.
Angels above and below.
Angels around you.
Angels assigned
To guard you wherever you go.

While I, my dearest,
In body and spirit,
Will wait for the day you come home.

WW

LITANIES

FOR SPECIAL OCCASIONS

THANKS AT SUPPERTIME
from Psalm 145

PREPARATION: *It will increase your closeness—to one another and to God—if you make a regular practice of specific thanksgivings. This is one of the most sacred ways of sharing the events of your separate days. Too, it will make your mealtime prayers more personal and more various.*

We suggest that each of you keep a diary of daily thanksgiving, in which to write—before the suppertime prayer—the gifts of God for which you are grateful. Learn to see the hand of God in the smallest encounters, the briefest of kindhearted gestures, the quickest moments of true gladness, and even in your own sudden acts of generosity. At the time of prayer, then, you will already have thought of God and the gifts. Date each entry so you can later refer to the actions of God and the changes they cause in you over the years.

(NOTE: This diary will become an invaluable part of the private retreat suggested later.)

The Litany

One after the other, let each partner pray the same formula, followed by your personal thanksgivings.

I WILL PRAISE YOU, MY GOD, and bless your name forever and ever. All your works do give you thanks; and all your saints do bless you, for you are faithful in all your words and gracious in all your deeds.

On this day, for these gifts, O Giver of every good thing, I offer my humble thanksgiving. Thank you for . . .

After both partners have named the gifts listed, let each conclude this portion of the prayer with:

Thank you for the one who eats with me here, for the house we share and the food we eat. Amen.

Then join together in the following words:

The eyes of all look to you, O Lord, and you give them their food in due season. You open your hand and satisfy the desire of every living thing. With our mouths we receive your goodness. With our mouths we praise you, too. Amen.

WW

THANKSGIVING FOR DAILY ACCOMPLISHMENTS

PREPARATION: Use this prayer at evening so that the blessings of the day can be remembered and acknowledged as gracious gifts from God. It may be prayed at the evening meal in the presence of other family members or privately between the two of you.

As you pray (you may take turns as readers), pause after each line so that each of you may name specific accomplishments of the day. For example, "a conflict resolved" may include a thanksgiving for coming to compromise with your teenage son about weekend curfews. A thanksgiving for "a project completed" may include a well-scrubbed bathroom.

Allow time for reflection at each line so that each of you has an opportunity to respond with thanksgivings for both your own and your partner's accomplishments.

The Litany

DEAR GOD, you give us the ability to accomplish good things in your name. Thank you for the blessings you have brought us today in these small accomplishments:

~ a success at work;
~ a project completed;
~ a task well done;

~ a conflict resolved;
~ a breakthrough in a relationship;
~ a hurdle overcome;
~ a battle won;
~ a fear conquered;
~ a test passed;
~ a need filled;
~ a lesson learned;
~ a lesson well taught.

Thank you for your guidance in these matters, Lord, and for providing the ability and wisdom to accomplish them well. We acknowledge your grace in these accomplishments, recognizing that it is only through you that we can do any good at all. Amen.

RW

THANKSGIVING FOR SPECIAL ACCOMPLISHMENTS

"If one member is honored, all rejoice together." (1 Cor. 12:26)

PREPARATION: *When one partner has accomplished something important, let the other one prepare for this glad litany, choosing a particular time and place and atmosphere.*

Find a keepsake, something that will hereafter signify the accomplishment. It needn't be expensive but should be meaningful and related to the person and the success.

Have ready a cup of thanksgiving and gladness, filled with something you may drink in a true celebration. Do you have special candles to indicate prayer and praise? Light them.

The Litany

Come together and follow this sequence:

1. *Name the accomplishment.*
2. *In your own words, speak your pride for your spouse's accomplishment.*
3. *But then say,* The Lord is our strength and our song. It is God who empowers the deeds of faithful people. God is the source of our talents and the praise in our accomplishments. Come, then, let's give our thanks to God, who establishes the work of our hands.

4. *Read aloud together Psalm 145; you read the odd verses, your spouse the even ones.*
5. *You, now, read 2 Corinthians 4:5-7, and discuss briefly how it applies to* this *accomplishment, whereby your hands and your hearts are lights shining for the glory of God.*
6. *Clasp hands together and pray:*

> O Majesty, how good you are to bring goodness into our house.
>
> Creator, you are our Father, you are our potter; we are the clay. We are the work of your hands; therefore, all we do is a grace from you and our praise returned to you.
>
> Thank you for joining us to divinity; for filling our small work with your greatness; for granting us the honor and the joy of personal achievement. And thank you for this marriage and a spouse with whom to share this good thing. Amen.

7. *Share the cup as a blessing to the Lord, saying:* Unto you, my Lord; and unto you, my love.
8. *Give your spouse the gift, the sign of sacred achievement.*
9. *Spend time softly talking together.*

WW

FOR THE SABBATH—AT ITS BEGINNING, AT ITS ENDING

PREPARATION: *This litany can surely be used on Sundays (especially if you make that day a sabbath—a day of genuine rest). But it will be a fruitful practice to use this litany as well before vacations or other periods of time set apart for rest, and thereby devoted to God our Creator.*

Bring candles that can stay lit a full day through.

Bring a Bible and pencils and, each of you, your "Sabbath book"—a notebook designed to last a while. At the appropriate moment in the litany, each will list in your own notebook the activities, the attitudes, the work that you give to God the Creator for the duration of this Sabbath. Think not only of activities related to your obvious jobs, but also of the worklike attitudes you take toward anything else in your life. Things done as duties need not, during the Sabbath, be done at all. The day of rest is also a day of trust: that God will oversee these things till you take them up again.

The Litany

Choose which of you will read A and which B, then follow this sequence:

At the beginning of Sabbath:

TOGETHER: Lord God, Creator of the Universe—

A: We, too, are creatures you have made.

TOGETHER: Lord God, Creator of the Universe—

B: You gave us the honor of work, of caring for creation.

TOGETHER: Lord God, Creator of the Universe—

A: But when you had finished your work, you rested.

TOGETHER: Lord God, Creator of the Universe—

B: And you commanded us to rest as well.

TOGETHER: This is our day of rest. We give the day and our faith to you. Amen.

A: *Read* Exodus 20:8-11. *End with the words:* Lord God, Creator of the Universe, today, by our glad and vigorous rest, we share with you the act of creation.

B: *Read* Deuteronomy 5:12-15. *End with the words:* Lord God, Redeemer of your people, by giving this day to you, we remember our bondage to sin and your salvation.

A: *Read* Mark 2:27.

B: *Read* Matthew 6:25-34.

TOGETHER: We beg you, Lord Jesus: fill our Sabbath rest with your peace.

1. *Let each of you now write in your Sabbath books today's date, under which you list the actions, the attitudes, the work that you give away to God this day.*
2. *Light the candles, one for each person involved. (These should stay lit all through the period of your Sabbath rest—except, of course, if you leave the house for a long time.)*
3. *Sing or speak these verses from the Isaac Watts hymn, "O God, Our Help in Ages Past":*

> O God, our Help in ages past, Our hope for years to come,
>   Our shelter from the stormy blast, And our eternal home!
>
> Under the shadow of Thy throne Thy saints have dwelt secure;
>   Sufficient is Thine arm alone, And our defense is sure.
>
> Before the hills in order stood Or earth received her frame,
>   From everlasting Thou art God, To endless years the same.
>
> O God, our Help in ages past, Our hope for years to come,
>   Be thou our Guard while troubles last And our eternal home. (LBW)

4. *Exchange Sabbath books. Let A read aloud the list of B; then let B read the list of A.*

5. *Spend a few minutes discussing how each of you will avoid the work you have given unto God, and spend this period of Sabbath time.*
6. *Together, clasp hands and pray:*

Lord, you have been our dwelling place through all generations, our protection, our home. Today we set time aside for your sake and for ours; we devote the time to you and to our rest; we separate it from our workaday world. We make it holy.

At the end of Sabbath:

Gather again at the candles. Clasp hands and pray, each in your own words, thanksgivings for the goodness of the Sabbath. Identify specifically what goodness was derived from the day.

A: God almighty, grant us a quiet night and peace at the last.

B: Guide us waking, O Lord, and guard us sleeping; that awake we may watch with Christ and asleep we may rest in peace.

TOGETHER: *Conclude by praying the Lord's Prayer, then extinguish the candles.*

WW

BEFORE BIBLE STUDY OR DEVOTIONS TOGETHER

PREPARATION: *In order to establish a regular time for devotions in your marriage, we suggest you make the following decisions together and that you establish a sacred covenant with one another to keep your choices as promises.*

Choose a time that you know can be honored, and then give it absolute priority, both for the sake of your faith and for the sake of your marriage.

Once a day is likely too often. Once a week is better, since this is God's time frame for worship and you will each have time to prepare in advance.

It need not be a weekend. It ought not be too late at night, since the flesh will overwhelm you then. Find a time when you both will be alert.

Identify both the beginning and the ending of your study, and obey both.

Choose a place that can, over time, feel sacred and welcoming to quiet meditation. Keep your books there. You might also prepare yourselves independently for devotions in that same place.

Keep diaries. If you aren't each keeping the diary of daily thanksgiving, which we describe on the pages of the "Thanks at Suppertime" litany, then let us suggest that you each keep a diary of weekly thanksgiving—a book in which you write down the good things God has done for you during the week previous to each devotion. Date the entries. And in the prayer at the end of your devotions, speak your genuine thanksgiving for God's gifts.

These diaries will be invaluable for the both of you when you choose to go on a private retreat together (see the final section of this book).

Establish a covenant together at the beginning of your first devotion. One at a time, speak solemn promises to your spouse that this time and this commitment will have priority in your lives. You will permit nothing to interrupt either your common devotions or your personal preparation for them.

Here is the place, here is the time, when God is most consciously invited to dwell within your formal relationship, the center of your minds and talk.

Bible study or devotions. We suggest that you alternate your practice from time to time.

Sometimes study individual books of the Bible on your own, then sometimes using materials or books prepared by others to guide your study. Don't neglect to study books on your own, since this will bring out interpretations most suited to the two of you; it can be an excellent opportunity for each to learn more of the faith of the other.

Sometimes let one of you lead the study and discussion, then exchange roles and let the other lead. If one of you feels less able, that one should work from the prepared material of others.

As time goes on, choose topics and lessons that speak to the immediate issues that marriage has raised between you.

Prayers. Always allow enough time at the end of the study for the spontaneous prayers of your hearts.

Conclude those prayers with the Lord's Prayer, and then, while laying hands each on the other, exchange the blessing that Paul used in his epistles: "The grace of our Lord Jesus Christ be with your spirit, [name your spouse]." Amen.

WW

A Prayer before Shared Bible Study or Devotions

But as for you, continue in what you have learned and have firmly believed, knowing from whom you learned it and how from childhood you have been acquainted with the sacred writings which are able to instruct you for salvation through faith in Christ Jesus. All scripture is inspired by God and is also profitable for teaching, for reproof, for correction, and for training in righteousness, that the child of God be complete, equipped for every good work. (2 Tim. 3:14-17)

PRAY TOGETHER: Jesus, you are our teacher and our master. Come, now, to open our eyes and enlighten our minds.

HUSBAND: Speak to me through the insights and wisdom of my wife; grant me the attention and the meekness to hear your word in her words.

WIFE: In the love of my husband let me know your love. In his knowledge let me know your will.

TOGETHER: Satisfy us together, Lord, for we together hunger and thirst for righteousness.

HUSBAND: I empty myself in order to receive your Spirit of Truth.

WIFE: I make my busy mind still for awhile, that you might dwell in it.

Now read Psalm 19 together, wife reading the odd verses, husband the even verses.

WW

ON AN ANNIVERSARY

PREPARATION: *Let each spouse think of two events in the past year that typify the character of the marriage. Describe these in writing. Bring the written words to this private celebration.*

If possible, let each of you find gifts that somehow betoken the events each remembers, whether one gift covers both or two gifts are needed.

Choose a particular time and place for the litany. It will be wonderful if this can be the same time and place every year.

The Litany

1. *Light candles that signify both the presence of God and your worship.*
2. *One after the other, each of you mark the forehead of your spouse with the sign of the cross, saying:* In the name of the Father, and of the Son, and of the Holy Spirit. *The spouse answers:* Amen. *Then read the following as indicated:*

TOGETHER: Lord God, you created us male and female. Now, by grace we have been married ____ years on this day.

WIFE: At our wedding, you heard and honored our vows to one another.

HUSBAND: Since then you've never left us. You have loved us and blessed us this last year, too.

WIFE: Thank you, dear Lord, for the gift of my husband, _____.

HUSBAND: Thank you, good Lord, for the gift of my wife, _____.

WIFE: You have protected him and strengthened him this year, too.

HUSBAND: You have comforted her and nourished her this year, too.

WIFE: In my husband, Jesus, I have seen your face.

HUSBAND: In my wife, Good Shepherd, I have heard your love.

3. *To each other, now, in your own plain words, speak your love.*
4. *One after the other, read the first of your memories from the previous year; then the second.*
5. *Exchange the gifts.*
6. *Now, praise the Lord for your years of marriage by reading together Psalm 150.*
7. *Finally, one of you read aloud the resurrection appearance of Jesus in Luke 24:28-35.*
8. *Following this, the other may pray:* O Lord Jesus, stay with us this next year, too. Whenever we sit to eat, bless the bread you've given us, and in the breaking of the bread, open our eyes to recognize you. Whenever we worship or study your Scriptures, cause our hearts to burn with love and the knowledge of you. And, Lord, use our marriage as a witness to your glorious resurrection. Amen.

WW

A YEARLY RETREAT
FOR RENEWAL

A YEARLY RETREAT

Background

AFTER AN ESPECIALLY DIFFICULT PATCH IN OUR MARRIAGE—when I was less than present for her and for the children—Thanne and I committed ourselves to a private retreat apart from home, the children, work, apart from everything except our relationship.

That first retreat turned out to be so important to us and to the whole rest of the year that we made it an annual practice.

Three days and two nights alone together, but with a structured pattern to our solitude: it became the sweet revival of our first covenant, of our quiet love, of our marriage. And it spread its blessing through half the year: three months before the trip, we were already looking forward to it; three months *after* the trip we continued to feel its blessing upon our daily, ordinary lives.

We recommend this to every couple, whatever your financial circumstances, whatever the age or complexity of your family. In fact, the more demanding and the more complex your family— *especially* if you have children—the more crucial will be this time apart.

Planning the Retreat

Long-term planning

Begin to plan your retreat almost a full year in advance. This means that shortly after one retreat is done, you are already making certain fixed decisions for the next.

Note: a retreat does *not* take the place of a family vacation. Nor is this an opportunity to visit anyone else, neither family nor friends. This is its own priority. Both of you must believe that this is an act necessary to the health of the marriage, not a concession to your spouse, not a mere "break" in routine, not an act whose significance is to be dismissed. Take it as seriously as any significant duty your job requires of you.

When? Establish the dates and keep them inviolate, unchangeable. Select three full days and two nights. (The schedule below shows the importance of devoting all three days entirely to this retreat.) Whether you choose a weekend or days midweek is up to you, of course; but Thanne and I found that the time was best during *off periods* of general travel and vacation. We chose midweek; we chose early spring or late autumn; and because our finances were nearly nonexistent, we were able to get cheaper rates in state park lodges during these seasons. We often found ourselves completely alone on hikes and in small restaurants.

How? Arrange now (as early as possible) to set yourselves free for these three days. It will ease your mind and keep the retreat from causing stress. If you work, get the time off well in advance. If you care for children, find someone who will commit to watching them.

Where? Choose the place of your retreat now. If necessary, book the three days. We suggest that you *don't* choose places where external activities might control your time or interfere with your attentions to one another and to the marriage. You must be in control of your time yourselves—although it is nice to have the option of pleasant activities nearby, things to do when you wish to do them. (As I mentioned, we went to state parks in Indiana and Kentucky. We also borrowed the cottages of friends; and once we took a room at a Benedictine monastery committed to hospitality. When we were able, we went to a motel in downtown Chicago.) There should be opportunity for you to spend time in various places, rooms, and environments that suit your activity and your mood.

As the time draws near

Each of you should accomplish certain private preparations, gathering and writing things that will serve the retreat and enrich the experience. Be sure to bring:

> ~ your diaries of daily thanksgiving (if one or both of you haven't been regularly writing in this book, then make a list of every good thing that happened in your lives—individual or together—during the last year; things seemingly insignificant are just as important as the big things);

~ a blessing cup;

~ your candles of devotion;

~ this book;

~ Bibles.

Let each of you, in a private preparation, recall and write down things you feel you did poorly in the past year, things you hope to improve with God's help (and the help of your spouse) in the year to come. Consider your habitual behavior, any particular event or action, your attitude, mood, care of self and others. This is about yourself, not your spouse; and it is for the *sake* of your spouse—who, likewise, is not listing your faults. Be absolutely honest.

Let each of you choose one important issue regarding your relationship to discuss while you're alone together. It may involve children; preparation for catastrophe; a dream you've been entertaining a while in your own soul; the writing or revision of your wills; insurance; job; house—absolutely anything that you feel requires the full attention of a lingering conversation together. Spend time making notes for the conversation so that you've truly thought it through.

Let each of you bring a gift to signify your recommitment to your spouse for this new year, too. We suggest you exchange these gifts at the very end of your second retreat day. To make that moment memorable, plan now (individually, secretly) how you will give the gift, with what gestures or words you will grant the moment a blessed romance.

A General Schedule (to review ahead of time)

Day 1

Use the morning of the first day—and the early portion of the afternoon, if necessary—to travel to the place of your retreat. We recommend that you are in place, checked in, unpacked and comfortable before supper of the first day.

That meal should be the self-conscious initiation of your retreat. And the evening that follows, though it won't be altogether *structured* by the activities of retreat, should nevertheless be devoted to the experience of "coming away to pray."

Day 2

Divide the second day into four parts: for (1) the morning and (2) the evening before bed, there should be specific prayers and activities. For the time between, you will decide how best to accommodate two separate discussions, with two separate topics—parts (3) and (4)—according to your own division of time.

The planned activities of your retreat should be interspersed with spontaneous activities of your own pleasure: walking, hiking, reading, board games, golf, going to a museum or ball game. Take advantage of the place where you are retreating. Whatever you choose to do for pleasure, however, we suggest that it be the choice and the genuine pleasure of you *both* and that it allow your attentions still to be on each other, permitting conversation, hand-holding, responsiveness one to the other, a genuine sense of personal intimacy.

Day 3

The third day is still a day completely devoted to your private time apart. The morning belongs to the place of your retreat. There should be no sense of urgency to return home, since the daily life ought not start till the following day. Pack to return and check out *after* a leisurely lunch.

In the afternoon or evening (as best suits you) travel home again, and gather (or meet) the children.

Conducting the Retreat

The First Day (prayer at departure)

This prayer for peace is one of the most ancient prayers of the Christian Church. It is at least 1,300 years old. When we pray it in private as our own, we stand in community with the countless multitudes of our faithful ancestors.

When the two of you are alone at the very beginning of your trip—in the car, at the airport—let one pray for the both of you:

Lord our God, from you come all holy desires, all good counsels, and all just works. Give us, your servants here, that peace which the world cannot give. Prepare our hearts to obey your commandments. Defend us from the fear of our enemies, so that we may pass these days in rest and in quietness. We pray in the name of—and through the merits of—Jesus Christ our Savior, who lives and reigns with you and the Holy Spirit, one God, world without end. Amen.

The First Day (suppertime)

The two of you are alone in a place permitting privacy, faith, and honesty. When you sit, before you eat, devote the food and these days apart and your hearts and your marriage to the Lord God. Use the following litany together with the Bible passages indicated. If you are inclined to do so, during supper you may discuss thoughts raised in your minds by the biblical passages. Let the wife read the A lines, the husband, the B lines.

A: Jesus, we've come to this place to be with each other and, together, to be with you.

B: Stay with us, O Lord. Bring peace to us as you brought it to your disciples after the resurrection.

A: Breathe upon us your truth and your comfort, as you breathed your Holy Spirit upon the disciples.

B: Let me hear you in the words of my wife.

A: Let me see you in the face of my husband.

B: We've come to this place to be with each other and, together, to be with you.

A: Blessed are those who hunger and thirst for righteousness, for they shall be satisfied.

B: *Read Isaiah 55:1-5.*

A: Blessed are the poor in spirit, for theirs is the kingdom of heaven. Blessed are the pure in heart, for they shall see God.

B: *Read Isaiah 55:6-9.*

A: Blessed are the merciful, for they shall obtain mercy. Blessed are the peacemakers, for they shall be called children of God.

B: *Read Isaiah 55:10-11.*

A: Blessed are those who mourn, for they shall be comforted. Blessed are the meek, for they shall inherit the earth.

B: *Read Isaiah 55:12-13.*

A: Stay with us, Lord Jesus. In these three days, enlighten our minds to you and toward one another.

TOGETHER: The eyes of all look to you, O Lord, and you give them their food in due season. You open your hand and satisfy the desire of every living thing. With our mouths we receive your goodness. With our mouths we will ever praise you, too. Amen.

The First Day (evening): "Great are the works of the Lord."

The dishes are done. You've relaxed a while. The candles that signal meditation are lit. You have your personal books of thanksgiving available. Maybe you're sipping something, and surely you are both in postures of lazy comfort, allowing the conversation that follows to be easy, ranging, casual. This time will be devoted to an assessment of blessings in the previous year.

1. Together read Psalm 111 slowly, with quiet contemplation. One of you read the odd verses, the other the even verses.

2. Now, together, go day by day through your diaries of daily thanksgiving. Discuss the year now past. Compare how some days seemed so different to each of you, while other days seemed exactly alike. Watch especially for the development of themes throughout the year. Can you, by this overview, see how God's hand was working in your lives even more than you were aware at the time?

What, then, do the two of you recognize now *for the first time* about God's care of you and his plans for you throughout the past year? Does this suggest anything about how you ought to live the coming year in order to acknowledge what he shows as important to your lives?

Note: If you haven't kept diaries of thanksgiving, you can nevertheless engage in this exercise by recalling specific dates—holidays, birthdays, your anniversary—and specific significant events of the previous year, and on the strength of your combined memories you can move through the year in quiet discussion, seeking the overview, the "forest" view of God's activity in your lives.

3. Can you together decide upon a particular word that most succinctly characterizes the year now finished? Or a symbol? Or a Bible story or passage?

When Israel, after wandering forty years in the wilderness, finally crossed the Jordan River into the promised land, God commanded that each tribe pick up a stone from the dried riverbed (Josh. 4:1-7). All twelve stones were then erected into a memorial in the midst of the Jordan, so that as the children and the grandchildren later passed by and saw the memorial, they would ask, "What do those stones mean?" The story of salvation could then be told over and over again, and never be forgotten.

Can the two of you think of a parallel to those stones—a word or symbol by which to characterize the previous year of your marriage? You might use a stone yourselves. Or you might create a picture, even a photograph, or a wall hanging—anything visible that can be added to year after year, so that when your children and your grandchildren ask about it you will be able to tell them all that God has continued to do in your marriage and your family. You can tell them the story that you two are living through right now.

4. End this glad retrospective with prayers of thanksgiving, each in your own words.

The Second Day (morning): "But there is forgiveness with thee."

After breakfast and after every small chore is done, sit down again in comfort for the following discussion, confession, and prayer. Each of you should have handy the list you made earlier about your personal failings in the previous year, the behavior you want to improve in the year to come.

Plan to spend anywhere from one to two hours on this exercise. Don't rush it; it takes a while to speak self-criticism out loud and accurately.

1. Light the candles and begin this period of self-assessment and forgiveness with the following prayer drawn from Psalm 5:

> **A:** Give ear to my words, O Lord; give heed to my groaning.
>
> **B:** Hearken to the sound of my cry, my King and my God, for to you I pray.
>
> **A:** O Lord, in the morning, now, you hear my voice.
>
> **B:** In the morning I prepare a sacrifice for you, and I watch.
>
> **A:** For you are not a God who delights in wickedness; evil may not live with you.
>
> **B:** The boastful may not stand before your eyes; you hate all evildoers.
>
> **A:** But I, through the abundance of your steadfast love, will enter your house. I will worship toward your holy temple in the fear of you.
>
> **B:** Lead me, O Lord, in your righteousness; make your way straight before me.

2. Establish a spiritual and mental context for confession by reading Psalm 130 aloud together. Note that this psalm is like a little four-act drama with two verses for each act. There is a reason why these four acts come in the sequence they do: they show how sinners feel and act when they stand before God seeking forgiveness. Discuss these four acts. What does each one mean for each of you?

3. Now, let spouse *A* confess his/her weaknesses of the past year. Speak them freely or, if spontaneous talk is difficult, read what you've written. Discuss them, if that helps. But there should be no judgment in that discussion (only God judges); there should be only a genuine search for understanding.

4. Next, spouse *B* asks several questions, to which spouse *A* gives true and faithful answers:

> **B:** Do you sincerely confess that you have sinned in various ways against God?
>
> **A:** Yes, I confess.
>
> **B:** Do you in your heart repent of your sins, committed in your thoughts, words, and deeds?
>
> **A:** Yes, I repent of my sins. All of them.
>
> **B:** Do you sincerely believe that God, by grace, for Jesus' sake, forgives all your sins?
>
> **A:** Yes, I believe in the love of God and in the salvation of Jesus Christ.
>
> **B:** Do you promise that you will with the help of the Holy Spirit improve your life and strive more and more to walk as Jesus walked?

A: Yes, I promise.

B: *Placing hands on the head of the confessing spouse, say with true conviction:* With the Lord our God there is steadfast love, and with him there is plenteous redemption. He redeems you from all your iniquities. The Lord Jesus forgives you. You are clean and pure. And I love you, too.

5. Now reverse roles and repeat this confession, letting spouse *B* speak his or her weaknesses, after which spouse *A* gives the blessing of forgiveness.

6. Together, now, discuss how each might help the other improve attitude and behavior in the year to come. This discussion needn't be completed now. Rather, allow it to run like a thread through the rest of these days and into the daily lives to which you will return.

7. Close this exercise with the following verses from Psalm 5:

A: Now let all who take refuge in you, O Lord, rejoice.

B: Let them sing for joy.

A: Defend them, O Lord, so that those who love you may exult in you.

B: For you bless the righteous; even now you are covering us with your favor as with a shield.

TOGETHER: *End by praying the Lord's Prayer.*

The Second Day (*morning to evening*)

Divide this day as suits you best—both to accommodate two separate discussions and to enjoy genuine relaxation and the time together. You can have these discussions while engaged in some other activity that allows you to pay full attention to one another, such as hiking, boating, walking a beach, eating in a restaurant, playing a game.

Or you may wish to separate entertainment from these discussions. It's up to you. But be sure to schedule the time committed to the discussions, perhaps up to an hour each. Be sure to put time and other activities between the discussions.

The two conversations that you hold now should revolve around the topics each of you chose earlier, in your private preparations for this retreat. Take each topic separately. Give each its full time and your full concentration. Neither of you should question why a topic was chosen or diminish its importance. And it isn't necessary to finish or solve anything now. What begins here may continue hereafter at home.

The Second Day (*evening, just before bed*)

The ending of this rich day together is a perfect time to renew your love for one another. We leave the words and the gestures and the shape of this activity totally up to the two of you. We suggest only this, that each of you shall have given thought to the *way* you will give your love the gift you've brought for him or her. Make it romantic according to your own personalities, your own histories.

And if you wish a biblical support to the delights of your body and the body of your spouse, read the Song of Solomon—the whole piece (which isn't long). Although this book of the Old Testament has often been interpreted to refer to the relationship between Jesus and the church, it is nonetheless a true love poem that delights in all the senses. Sometimes the young man speaks; sometimes the young woman speaks. You might select passages to read to one another.

The Third Day (morning worship)

On this last morning before returning home, your attention is drawn to the relationship between God and the church. The images of bride and bridegroom, husband and wife, point to marriage as the bond most closely resembling the covenant relationship between God and his people.

For this time of closure, sit facing each other if possible. Then light candles, signifying God's presence.

Between each scripture reading and prayer, allow some time of silence to reflect on the reading. One of you may read the scripture, the other the short prayers that follow. Read together where it is indicated.

TOGETHER: We go today from this place, bound together by God's love, our love for each other, and renewed commitment to our marriage.

TOGETHER: Come, Lord Jesus, be our guest.

TOGETHER: *Read Psalm 133.*

TOGETHER: We praise you for this marriage, for binding us together in a unity that overflows with blessing.

A: *Read* Isaiah 54:4-8.

B: We praise you for your compassion and mercy. Just as you put away the sins of your people, empower each of us to put away the sins of the other in our marriage.

A: *Read* Isaiah 62:1-5.

B: We praise you for creating marriage at the very beginning of all time when all of your creation was pronounced "good." Just as you delighted in your people, delight also in this union.

B: *Read* Jeremiah 2:2-3.

A: We praise you for your protection of our marriage covenant. Just as Israel followed you in her youth, teach us to follow you.

B: *Read* Hosea 2:14-23.

A: We praise you for your "yes" to us when we stray from you and away from our marriage covenant. Just as you wooed Israel back to you and pronounced again that she was your people and you were her God, enable each of us to woo back the other when one of us has sinned.

B: *Read* Revelations 19:6-8.

A: We praise you that you are preparing now to receive us as your bride. Just as your bride is adorned with the fine linen of righteous deeds, clothe us with your righteousness as we adorn ourselves for each other.

B: *Read* Revelations 21.

A: We praise you for this glimpse of your bride, the holy city—Jerusalem. Just as you make all things new and shine with the radiance of rare jewels, renew our marriage so that it reflects your glory.

TOGETHER: Go with us now from this place.

A: Strengthen the ties that bind us together.

B: Tighten the bond when it loosens.

A: Walk before us into the future and lead us in your ways.

B: Lift us when we stumble.

A: Put away our past sins and clothe us with your righteousness.

B: Restore us when we fail.

TOGETHER: Together we commit ourselves to you, Lord.

A: And I commit myself to you, [name], in the name of Jesus.

B: And I commit myself to you, [name], in the name of Jesus.

TOGETHER: Stay with us now as together we await your final coming to receive us as your bride. Amen, it shall be so.

TOGETHER: *Read* Psalm 100.

Extinguish the candles and go on your way in peace.

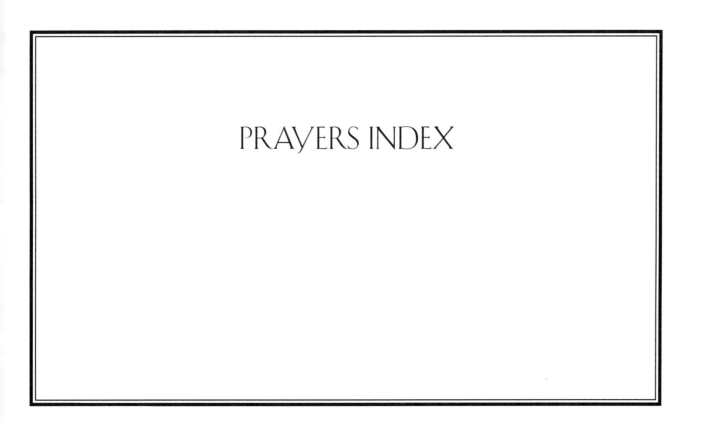

PRAYERS INDEX

PRAYERS INDEX
When you want to pray about . . .